RAWMAZING DESSERTS

RAWMAZING
DESSERTS

DELICIOUS AND EASY RAW FOOD RECIPES FOR COOKIES,
CAKES, ICE CREAM, AND PIE

SUSAN POWERS

Skyhorse Publishing

ACKNOWLEDGMENTS

To my daughters, Mia and Kaia: I couldn't be more proud of you both. You are a constant inspiration for me to live my best life. To my father, Phillip Powers: Though he hasn't been with us for more than 30 years, his inspirational, forward thinking planted the seeds that have led me on my journey to seek health through nutrition and lifestyle. To my mother, Cora, for her help in the kitchen and for being a willing tester and supporter. To Amy Oscar your patience, sharp eye and beautiful wordsmithing are an amazing gift. To Peter, your support of me and belief in me is so inspiring. And finally, to everyone who is interested in living a healthier life, starting with their plate.

Contents

When I introduce people to Rawmazing—the raw food lifestyle—for the first time, I start with dessert. The response is always the same: "This is raw? This is healthy?"

I can understand their surprise. All of their lives, they've been offered high-calorie desserts containing white sugar, white flour, eggs, cream, and butter. Their sweet tooth has been trained to expect the taste of processed food—almost all of which contains high-fructose corn syrup. Not exactly high on the good-for-you food list!

"Wow!" their faces telegraph when I show them how to combine almonds, avocados, agave, and cacao powder in a food processor and turn out a creamy, rich chocolate mousse, or when I serve them a slice of "cheesecake" that looks like it came off the shelf at the best bakery but is, in fact, raw, vegan, and made only from fruits, nuts, and agave.

No wonder they're amazed when they learn they can enjoy rich, delicious desserts made of the healthiest foods on Earth; nutrient-dense ingredients like fruits and nuts, with dates for sweetening and unprocessed cacao for heart health! When even your dessert provides you with antioxidants, vitamins, phytonutrients, and minerals, the picture of what a Rawmazing lifestyle might look like starts to change.

Rawmazing desserts are pure delight—literally. They taste better than their traditional counterparts because they're made with real, whole, healthy ingredients that our bodies were made to eat. Even better, there's no bloating, lethargy, or guilt when you're finished eating a raw dessert—only energy, lightness, and the joy of knowing that while treating your taste buds, you've given your body the gift of deep-tissue nutrition.

When you see how easy Rawmazing desserts are to prepare—even a beginner home cook can whip together a gourmet dessert in minutes—you'll be hooked, and on your way to living a Rawmazing life!

— Susan Powers

Susan Powers

My Thoughts on Dessert

I have always loved desserts—and growing up in a family of fabulous cooks established my sweet tooth at an early age. I'd stand on a stool beside my Grandmother Ola, learning how to sift the flour and mix the ingredients to make the cookies I so loved. I still remember my mother's patience as she taught me her special recipes and—since the kitchen often looked like a tornado had gone through after I was done—tried to get me to clean up as I worked. I still love making, and eating, desserts. But I'm no longer interested in the nutrient-empty desserts of my youth. Oh, I still want the treats—but I want them to be healthy and beautiful and, in the Rawmazing tradition, easy to make!

That said, please keep in mind that raw desserts are nutritious but can be calorie dense. They are desserts and should be treated as such. Servings are smaller than traditional desserts—and should be served like any dessert, as a special treat to round out a healthy meal.

BREADS & BISCOTTI

Dehydration

All dehydration times are suggested times. When dehydrating, many variables come into play, such as air humidity and the type of dehydrator used. Though I offer guidelines in the recipes in this cookbook—and on Rawmazing.com—I always check as I go.

I am often asked: Why do you start the dehydration at a higher temperature and then lower it? To maintain the integrity of raw food, the *food* temperature must not get above 118°F. When food is still in the wet state, the temperature is much lower than the air temperature. By starting at a higher temperature, you can reduce the moisture in the food more quickly, reducing dehydration times and also preventing fermentation.

Note: I always set a timer to remind myself to turn the temperature down after the first initial drying time.

Zucchini Bread

This bread is moist with a beautiful crumb-like texture, much like traditional baked zucchini breads. To ensure moist texture, take care not to overdehydrate.

Makes 2 loaves

Ingredients:
2 Apples
¼ cup Agave Nectar
3 cups Almond Flour
½ cup Ground Flax Seeds
1 tablespoon Cinnamon
4 cups Shredded Zucchini
1 cup Chopped Walnuts (optional)

Instructions:
1. Core and quarter apples. Place in food processor with agave. Process until smooth.
2. Mix together almond flour, flax seed, and cinnamon.
3. Mix together apple mixture and zucchini. Add to dry ingredients. Stir until combined.
4. Stir in walnuts.
5. Pat mixture into 2 loaves, no more than 1-inch high.
6. Dehydrate at 140°F for 1 hour, reduce heat, and dehydrate for 5 hours.
7. Slice into 1-inch slices and continue to dehydrate until dry.

Step 3 · Step 5 · Step 7

Tropical Biscotti

This is a moist dough—yielding a drier, crunchy cookie—so don't be surprised if it takes longer than other breads to dehydrate.

Makes 1 dozen

Ingredients:
½ cup Dried Apricots, chopped
½ cup Dried Pineapple, chopped
1 cup Ground Almonds
1½ cups Almond Flour
1 cup Dried Coconut
½ cup Agave Nectar
½ cup Currants
1 large Orange, juice and zest from

Instructions:
1. Hand chop apricots and pineapple, and set aside.
2. Separately process 1 cup almonds in food processor.
3. Add almond flour and coconut. Pulse until just combined.
4. Add agave and pulse until combined. Remove from processor and place in bowl.
5. Add orange juice and zest, combine by hand. Mix in chopped fruit and currants.
6. Form into biscotti-shaped loaves and dehydrate 8 hours.
7. Cut into ¾-inch slices, return to dehydrator, and dehydrate until very dry.

Step 5

Step 6

Step 7

Cherry Almond Biscotti

A beautiful way to start your day, these are bursting with flavor and very easy to make. The texture is a little chewier than baked biscotti. Please note the almond extract is not raw.

Makes 1 dozen

Ingredients:
1 cup Almonds, chopped fine in food processor
1½ cups Almond Flour
¹/₃ cups Coconut Oil, softened
½ cup Agave Nectar
1 cup Dried Coconut, unsweetened
2 teaspoons Almond Extract
1 cup Dried Cherries, chopped

Instructions:
1. Mix all ingredients together.
2. Form into long loaf, ½-inch thick.
3. Dehydrate at 140°F for 30 minutes, then at 116°F for 3 hours.
4. Cut into slices and dehydrate until very dry, 4–6 more hours.

Ingredients

Step 2

Cacao Pecan Biscotti

Not too sweet and loaded with antioxidants and nutrients. The cacao and pecans combine to make a crisp, delicious biscotti for a coffee break or anytime of the day!

Makes 16 biscotti

Ingredients:
1 cup Almond Flour
1 cup Raw Oat Flour
½ cup Cacao Powder
$1/3$ cup Coconut Butter, softened
$1/3$ cup Agave Nectar
¼ cup Water, filtered
1 cup Pecans, chopped

Instructions:
1. Mix together almond flour, oat flour, and cacao powder.
2. Whisk together coconut butter, agave nectar, and water.
3. Stir wet ingredients into dry ingredients.
4. Pat mixture into a ½-inch thick rectangular log measuring about 5x13 inches.
5. Dehydrate at 145°F for ½ hour, reduce temperature to 116°F, and dehydrate for 3 hours.
6. Slice into ½-inch pieces. Dehydrate until dry.

Buying Seasonally

As I write this it's July and the local Farmer's Markets are in full swing. I am in heaven as I can run down any day and get fresh, just-picked seasonal produce at great prices. When I make desserts, I try to make the recipes that use the freshest local fruit. Right now, raspberries are in season and I am taking full advantage of using and freezing raspberries so I can make Raspberry Sorbet and other raspberry desserts throughout the year!

Not only does it save money to shop in season, but also by choosing local produce whenever possible, the flavors are delightful! I buy extra in-season fruits and veggies and freeze them for later use—an economical way to enjoy local food year-round.

COOKIES

Chocolate, Chocolate Chip Cookies
Lemon Raspberry Cookies
Oatmeal Raisin Cookies
Cacao Walnut and Vanilla Macaroons
Glazed Lemon Chia Seed Macaroons

"TOASTING" NUTS

If you want your nuts to be more flavorful, throw them in the dehydrator for an hour before you put them in your recipe. The heat helps the oils start to release and makes the nuts very tasty!

Chocolate, Chocolate Chip Cookies

This cookie has a traditional baked cookie-like texture and a wonderful, satisfying chocolate taste. Kids love them! (As always, nuts are optional.)

Makes 2 dozen small cookies

Ingredients:
1 cup Zucchini
1/3 cup Agave Nectar
½ cup Coconut Butter, softened
1 cup Raw Oat Flour
½ cup Cacao Powder
½ teaspoon Cinnamon
1½ cups Raw Flaked Oats
½ cup Chopped Walnuts (optional)
½ cup Cacao Nibs (optional)

Instructions:
1. Combine zucchini puree (simply puree zucchini in your food processor), agave, and coconut butter in food processor. Blend well.
2. Mix together oat flour, cacao powder, and cinnamon.
3. Stir in wet mixture. Combine well.
4. Stir in raw oats, optional walnuts, and optional cacao nibs. Mix well.
5. Press into cookie shapes and dehydrate for 30 minutes at 140°F. Reduce heat and dehydrate for 4–5 more hours at 115°F.

Lemon Raspberry Cookies

I love these little cookies! They look as if they came right out of a pastry case!

Note: You will need to spend a little time with the high-speed blender and the plunger as it takes some work to get the beautiful, smooth consistency for the filling. The extra effort is well worth it!

Makes 2 dozen small cookies

Cookies Ingredients:

1 cup Almonds

2 cups Dried Coconut

¼ cup Coconut Butter, softened

¼ cup Agave Nectar

¼ cup Maple Syrup*

1 pint Fresh Raspberries

*Maple syrup is not raw but used in raw food making

Filling:

1 cup Cashews, soaked until soft (at least 4 hours)

$^1/_3$ cup Coconut Butter, softened

½ cup Lemon Juice

2 Lemons, zest from

Pinch of Salt

½ teaspoon Vanilla Extract

2 teaspoons Nutritional Yeast

Cookies Instructions:

1. Soak almonds, remove skins, and process in food processor until ground fine.
2. Mix together with other ingredients.
3. Using a 2-inch baking ring, place the ring on the nonstick sheet, put a tablespoon of dough in the ring, and press firmly. Lift the ring, and you will have the cookie shape.
4. Dehydrate at 140°F for 30 minutes; reduce the dehydration temperature to 116°F. Dehydrate until dry. Halfway through dehydration process, remove cookies from nonstick sheet and move to mesh sheet so they can properly dry.

Filling Instructions & Assembly:

1. Drain cashews.
2. Combine all ingredients in a high-speed blender and blend until smooth.
3. Pipe filling onto cookies and top with a raspberry.

Cookies, Step 3

21

Oatmeal Raisin Cookies

These are quick, simple, super-healthy cookies that are great to have around for surprise snack attacks. Another kid's favorite!

Makes 2 dozen small cookies

Ingredients:
3 medium Apples
2 cups Raw Flaked Oats
1 cup Raw Oat Flour
½ cup Coconut Oil, softened
¼ cup Agave Nectar
1 tablespoon Cinnamon
1 cup Raisins

Instructions:
1. Make the apple puree: quarter and core apples, leaving the peel on. Process in food processor until pureed.
2. In a separate bowl, stir together oats and oat flour.
3. Stir in remaining ingredients, in order.
4. Drop in mounds onto nonstick sheets. Flatten slightly.
5. Place in dehydrator for 45 minutes at 145°F, remove from nonstick sheets, and place on screen. Continue dehydrating at 115°F for 6–8 hours or until almost dry.

Step 1

Step 3

Step 4

Cacao Walnut and Vanilla Macaroons

I made these one day when I was craving chocolate chip and walnut cookies.
They are rich and tasty, and both vegan and gluten-free.

Makes 2 dozen small cookies

Ingredients:
2 cups Dried Coconut, unsweetened
½ cup Almond Flour
$^1/_3$ cup Cacao Powder
¼ cup Coconut Butter
¼ cup Maple Syrup
¼ cup Agave Nectar
1 Vanilla Bean (the scraped insides)
1 cup Walnuts, chopped

Instructions:
1. In large mixing bowl, combine all ingredients except walnuts.
2. Stir in walnuts.
3. Shape into balls and dehydrate at 115°F for 4–5 hours.

For the Vanilla Macaroons, omit cacao and walnuts.

Ingredients

Step 1

Step 3

Glazed Lemon Chia Seed Macaroons

Reminiscent of your favorite lemon and poppy seed recipes, these cookies are filled with the added nutritional punch of chia seeds! Topped with a lemon glaze, they'll satisfy your cookie craving!

Makes ½ dozen

Cookies Ingredients:
3 cups Dried Coconut, unsweetened
1½ cups Almond Flour
½ cup Chia Seeds
1 Lemon, juice and zest from
¼ cup Agave Nectar
¼ cup Maple Syrup
¼ cup Coconut Butter

Lemon Glaze:
$^1/_3$ cup Coconut Butter
2 tablespoons Agave Nectar
4 tablespoons Lemon Juice
1 Lemon, zest from

Cookies Instructions:
1. Stir together dried coconut, almond flour, and chia seeds.
2. Whisk together lemon juice, lemon zest, agave, maple syrup, and coconut butter.
3. Mix wet ingredients into dry ingredients. Combine well.
4. Shape into cookies and place on dehydrator screens.
5. Dehydrate at 145°F for ½ hour, decrease heat, and dehydrate at 116°F until dry, approximately 8 hours.
6. Cool.

Lemon Glaze Instructions:
1. Whisk all ingredients together.

Assembly:
1. Dip tops of cookies in glaze, refrigerate to set.

SOAKING NUTS

Some nuts, like cashews, are soaked for texture and for the moisture this brings to a recipe. Other nuts, such as almonds and walnuts, should be presoaked to release enzyme inhibitors. I always soak nuts for 8 hours when I first get them; then I dehydrate them until dry. That way I always have soaked nuts on hand for a recipe. If I need "wet" nuts for a recipe, I simply resoak them.

CAKES & CUPCAKES

Cacao Ganache Mousse Cake
Ginger Peach Torte
Orange Chocolate Cheesecake
Strawberry Shortcake
Chocolate Cupcakes
Brownie Bites

ALMOND FLOUR

There are a few different ways to make almond flour. You can soak your almonds (to release the enzyme inhibitors, see Soaking Nuts), dehydrate them, and then grind fine. This will make a coarser flour. The second method is to dehydrate the leftover pulp from making almond milk. I always save my pulp and dehydrate it right away. After it is dry, you can use a coffee grinder or high-speed blender to process into a powder. This yields a lighter, finer almond flour.

Cacao Ganache Mousse Cake

Reminiscent of a flourless chocolate cake with a chocolate mousse filling and rich ganache frosting! The results will amaze you and your friends!

Serves 6–8

Cake Ingredients:
3 cups Almond Flour
1½ cups Oat Flour
1 cup Cacao Powder
¾ cup Water, filtered
¾ cup Coconut Butter, softened
½ cup Maple Syrup
½ cup Agave Nectar

Mousse Filling:
1 Vanilla Bean
2 cups Cashews, soaked
1 Young Thai Coconut, flesh and liquid
¾ cup Coconut Butter, softened
$^1/_3$ cup Agave Nectar
½ cup Cacao Powder

Chocolate Ganache:
See full instructions on page 115

Cake Instructions:
1. Oil and line three 6-inch round cake pans with parchment.
2. Combine dry ingredients: almond flour, oat flour, and cacao powder; mix well.
3. Combine wet ingredients: water, coconut butter, maple syrup, and agave.
4. Stir together until combined. Don't overmix.
5. Press cake "batter" into pans.
6. Dehydrate for 1 hour at 140°F, then reduce heat to 115°F and dehydrate for 8 hours.
7. Remove from cake pans, peel off parchment, and set aside.

Mousse Filling Instructions:
1. Split the vanilla bean, scrape out the insides, and set aside.
2. Place all ingredients in the food processor or high-speed blender and blend until very smooth and fluffy.
3. Refrigerate for at least 1 hour to firm up.

Assembly:
1. Make ganache.
2. Spread refrigerated filling between three cake layers. You want about an inch of filling.
3. Place cake on a rack with parchment or waxed paper underneath; the wax paper will catch drips. Make sure the cake is straight.
4. Slowly pour ganache over the top of the cake. Refrigerate to set ganache.

Ginger Peach Torte

A delight for the palate, this beautiful ginger cake layered with a peach and whipped "cream" filling creates a dreamy taste explosion. Light yet dense, this is one of my favorite recipes.

Serves 8–10

Cake Ingredients:

3 cups Almond Flour

1½ cups Raw Oat Flour

1 teaspoon Cinnamon

2 teaspoons Powdered Ginger

¾ cup Coconut Butter, softened

½ cup Water

½ cup Agave Nectar

½ cup Maple Syrup

Filling:

2 cups Cashew Whipped Cream (see page 119)

4 ripe peaches, peeled, halved, and sliced

Topping:

½ cup Pecans, chopped (optional)

Cake Instructions:

1. Mix together almond flour and oat flour.

2. Stir in cinnamon and ginger.

3. In a separate bowl, whisk together coconut butter, water, agave, and maple syrup.

4. Stir wet ingredients into dry ingredients.

5. Place mixture in two 6 inch round cake pans, lined with oiled parchment.

6. Dehydrate for 1 hour at 145°F. Reduce heat to 116°F and dehydrate for 4 more hours.

7. Remove from pans and dehydrate at 116°F until almost dry.

Filling Instructions:

1. Fold peaches into whipped "cream."

Assembly:

1. Spread half of filling between cake layers.

2. Top with the other half of the filling.

3. Sprinkle chopped pecans on top, if desired.

Orange Chocolate "Cheese" Cake

Serves 12

Crust Ingredients:

1/2 cup Almonds

1/2 cup Pecans

4 Dates, soaked until soft

1/4 cup Cacao Powder

Filling Ingredients:

1/2 cup Orange zest

2 cups Cashews, soaked until soft (4+ hours), rinsed and drained well

1 1/4 cup Coconut Oil, melted

1 cup fresh Orange juice (approx. 3 oranges, depending how juicy they are)

2/3 cup raw Agave Nectar

1 tablespoon Ginger, grated

Crust Instructions:

1. Place almonds and pecans in food processor and process until finely chopped.

2. Add dates and cacao. Process until well blended. Mixture should stick together when you pinch it.

3. Press 2/3 of the mixture into the bottom of a 7-inch spring form pan.

lined with parchment paper. Make sure you press it well.

4. Set the remaining 1/3 mixture aside to use for filling layer or to sprinkle on top.

Filling Instructions:

1. Zest oranges and set aside.

2. In high-speed blender, combine cashews, coconut oil, orange juice and raw agave nectar. Blend until smooth.

3. Add zest and ginger. Pulse just to combine.

4. Pour over crust.

5. Refrigerate overnight.

6. Top with remaining crust.

Chef's Note: If you want to use the crust as a layer (like photo), you will need to pour half the filling mixture into the pan and place it in the freezer for a bit (DO NOT LET IT FREEZE) to let it set up. Sprinkle crust over bottom layer then carefully pour in the remaining filling mixture.

Use Spring Form Pan

Crust: Step 4

Filling: Step 4

Strawberry Shortcake

A delightful raw translation of the traditional strawberry shortcake.

Serves 4

Cake Ingredients:
1¼ cups Almond Flour
2 cups Raw Oat Flour
2 cups Strawberries
½ cup Coconut Butter, softened
½ cup Agave Nectar

Filling:
1 cup Cashew Whipped Cream
   (see page 119)
1 cup Strawberries, sliced

Sauce:
1 cup Strawberries
¼ cup Agave Nectar

Cake Instructions:
1. Mix together almond flour and oat flour.
2. Puree strawberries in food processor.
3. Add coconut butter and agave. Pulse until combined.
4. Stir wet ingredients into dry ingredients.
5. Place four oiled 5-inch molds on nonstick sheet.
6. Distribute batter between molds.
7. Dehydrate for 1 hour at 145°F. Reduce heat to 116°F and dehydrate for 4 more hours.
8. Remove rings and dehydrate until dry but still a little moist. If you press on the top, it will not be gooey or hard.

Filling Instructions:
1. Fold sliced strawberries into whipped cream.

Sauce Instructions:
1. Blend well.

Assembly:
1. Place small cake on plate.
2. Top with filling.
3. Pour strawberry sauce on top.

Chocolate Cupcakes

These are fabulous: dense chocolate with a cake-like consistency, they're a great treat for everyone!

Makes 6 servings

Cake Ingredients:

3 cups Almond Flour

1½ cups Oat Flour

1 cup Cacao Powder

¾ cup Water, filtered

¾ cup Coconut Butter, softened

½ cup Maple Syrup

½ cup Agave Nectar

Frosting:

2 cups Cashews, soaked at least 3 hours until soft

½ cup Agave Nectar

⅓ cup Coconut Butter, softened

Natural Food Coloring (optional)

Cake Instructions:

1. Combine dry ingredients: almond flour, oat flour, and cacao powder; mix well.

2. Combine wet ingredients: water, coconut butter, maple syrup, and agave.

3. In a separate bowl, stir wet and dry ingredients together until combined. Don't overmix.

4. Using paper muffin cups (you will need these to prevent sticking) or silicone cupcake shells, fill to the top.

5. Dehydrate for 1 hour at 140°F, then reduce heat to 115°F and dehydrate for 8 hours.

Frosting Instructions:

1. Combine all ingredients in high-speed blender or food processor. Process until very smooth.

Brownie Bites

Everyone loves brownies! And now, with these chewy chocolate delights—you can love them raw!

Makes 1 dozen

Ingredients:
3 cups Almond Flour
1½ cups Oat Flour
1 cup Cacao Powder
¾ cup Water, filtered
¾ cup Coconut Butter, softened
½ cup Maple Syrup
½ cup Agave Nectar

Instructions:
1. Combine almond flour, oat flour, and cacao powder.
2. Whisk together water, coconut butter, maple syrup, and agave.
3. Stir together dry mixture and wet mixture.
4. Press into mini-cupcake muffin papers.
5. Dehydrate for 1 hour at 140°F, then reduce heat to 115°F and dehydrate for 8 hours.

Raw Oat Flour & Raw Flaked Oats

I was at our local organic farmers market when I first met Darrold and Marty Glanville. Marty was putting raw, organic oat groats in this little "flaker," turning the handle, and producing raw flaked oats! You can imagine how that caught my attention. A way to finally start including oats and oat flour that was organic and raw!

Darrold is passionate about sourcing grain. He travels all over the United States and Canada looking for organic, heritage grains. I love his commitment and dedication. (See resources for more information.)

CUSTARDS & MOUSSES

Fruit Parfait
Blueberry Peach Chia Pudding
Lemon Glazed Fruit and Custard
Hazelnut Chocolate Mousse

Fruit Parfait

This is a refreshing dessert when something lighter but still decadent is wanted. Beautiful and great for entertaining!

Serves 4

Fruit:
1 cup Strawberries, sliced
1 cup Blueberries
1 cup Bananas, sliced

Vanilla Cream:
1 Vanilla Bean
2 cups Cashews, soaked until soft
1 Young Thai Coconut, flesh and ¼ cup liquid
¾ cup Coconut Butter, softened
½ cup Agave Nectar

Chocolate Ganache:
See full instructions on page 115

Vanilla Cream Instructions:
1. Split vanilla bean and scrape out insides with tip of knife.
2. Add to all other ingredients and process in a high-speed blender until smooth.
3. You will have to be patient to get a smooth consistency. Refrigerate 2 hours.

Fruit Parfait Assembly:
1. Toss fruit together.
2. Transfer fruit to individual serving glasses or plates, alternating layers of fruit, vanilla cream, and chocolate ganache.

Blueberry Peach Chia Pudding

I was always a big fan of tapioca pudding. Loved the texture, the taste, the richness. I still love contrasts—and this pudding is full of them. I wanted an extra-rich pudding, so I used cashew cream instead of milk. Topped off with a delightful combination of peaches and blueberries, it makes a great dessert. Chia Seeds are a super food!

Makes 4 cups

Ingredients:
1¾ cups Cashew Cream (see page 117 for recipe)
½ cup Chia Seeds
½ cup Agave Nectar
1 teaspoon Vanilla
½ teaspoon Cinnamon
1 cup Peaches
1 cup Blueberries

Instructions:
1. Mix together cashew cream, chia seeds, agave, vanilla, and cinnamon. Set aside.
2. Cut peaches.
3. When chia pudding has thickened up (about 5–10 minutes), stir in sliced peaches and blueberries.
4. Keep refrigerated.

Lemon Glazed Fruit and Custard

Light as a cloud with the perfect summer combination of lemon and fresh berries.

Serves 4

Vanilla Custard:
1 Vanilla Bean
2 cups Cashews, soaked until soft
1 Young Thai Coconut, flesh and ¼ cup liquid
¾ cup Coconut Butter
½ cup Agave Nectar

Toppings:
1 cup Blueberries
1 cup Strawberries
1 Orange, zest from

Lemon Glaze:
¼ cup Coconut Butter
2 tablespoons Agave Nectar
1 tablespoon Lemon Juice
1 Lemon, zest from

Vanilla Custard Instructions:
1. Split vanilla bean and scrape out insides.
2. Add insides of vanilla bean to all other ingredients and process in high-speed blender until smooth.
3. Refrigerate.

Lemon Glaze:
1. Mix all ingredients together. This will set up fast so make it at the last minute.
   If it thickens, gently warm to get it back to a pourable state.

Assembly:
1. Place 2 or 3 spoonfuls of custard on plate.
2. Top with berries. Spoon lemon glaze over top.
3. Sprinkle with orange zest.

Hazelnut Chocolate Mousse

You will be surprised and delighted by the flavor and creamy consistency of this decadent mousse. Nutella lovers will be in Heaven.

Serves 4

Ingredients:
2 Avocados
½ cup Hazelnut Butter
1 cup Hazelnut Milk
¾ cup Cacao Powder
½ cup Agave Nectar

Hazelnut Butter:
2 cups Hazelnuts (not soaked, dry)
2 tablespoons Olive Oil

Hazelnut Milk:
1 cup Hazelnuts
3 cups Water

Hazelnut Butter Instructions:
1. Follow instructions for Almond Butter on page 99.
2. Hazelnut butter takes longer and you will want to add a little olive oil toward the end of processing.

Hazelnut Milk Instructions:
1. Place hazelnuts and water in high-speed blender. Blend very well.
2. Strain through nut milk bag or several layers of cheesecloth.

Mousse Instructions:
1. Place all ingredients in food processor.
2. Process until very smooth. Refrigerate before serving.
3. Top with grated hazelnuts if desired.

Step 1

Nut Milk Bag

Enjoy

PIES & TARTS

White & Dark Chocolate Raspberry Tort
Banana Cream Tart with Walnut Crust
Pecan Pie
Apple Pie
Strawberry Coconut Cream Pie
Chocolate Raspberry Ganache Tart

Pans, Tart Pans & Springform Pans

There are quite a few different pans, tart pans, and springform pans that I use when making these desserts. The tart pans come in many sizes. I seem to gravitate to 8-inch, 6-inch, and also 4 ½-inch. They all have fluted sides and removable bottoms.

I also have 8-inch and 6-inch springform pans. These have sides that actually tighten around the base. Once the dessert is done, you just loosen the top and unmolding is easy—a necessity for cheesecakes.

Another pan I use is the traditional cupcake pan, both large and small. You will need liners as raw desserts do not drop out as easily as traditional baked ones. I also have used silicone molds. I find them wonderful to work with for both cupcakes and fudge when I want a particular shape.

White & Dark Chocolate Raspberry Torte

Inspired by a torte that I used to make in the "old days," this torte is sinful in taste and appearance but not in ingredients. With its white chocolate, dark chocolate, and raspberry combination, this one's for your best dinner party.

Serves 10–12

Chocolate Crust Ingredients:
1½ cups Almonds, finely ground
¼ cup Cacao Powder
2 tablespoons Coconut Oil, softened

Filling:
2 cups Cashews, soaked
$^1/_3$ cup Agave Nectar
½ cup Cacao Butter, melted
$^1/_3$ cup Coconut Oil, melted
1 teaspoon Vanilla
2 pints Raspberries

Chocolate Crust Instructions:
1. Combine finely ground almonds with cacao powder and coconut butter.
2. Press into an 8-inch tart pan with removable bottom.
3. Refrigerate.

Filling Instructions:
1. Blend cashews, agave, cacao butter, coconut oil, and vanilla in food processor.
2. Process until very smooth. You can also use a high-speed blender.
3. Spread a thin layer of filling on the crust.
4. Place a layer of raspberries over the filling. Pack them tightly.
5. Pour the rest of the filling mixture over raspberries.
6. Refrigerate. Top with layer of Chocolate Ganache (see page 115 for recipe).

Banana Cream Tart with Walnut Crust

I love banana cream pie. This raw version is healthy, tasty, and even has a raw chocolate topping.

Serves 4–6

Crust Ingredients:
1½ cups Walnuts
1 cup Brazil Nuts
5 Pitted Dates, soaked until soft
2 tablespoons Coconut Butter, softened

Filling:
2 cups Cashews, soaked at least 3 hours
1 cup Young Thai Coconut, flesh from
¼ cup Coconut Water (from fresh coconut)
1 teaspoon Lemon Juice
¼ cup Agave Nectar
¼ cup Coconut Butter, softened
1 Vanilla Bean
2 Bananas

Raw Chocolate:
1 cup Raw Cacao Butter
3 tablespoons Coconut Oil
1 teaspoon Vanilla Extract
7 ounces Cacao Powder
$^1/_3$ cup Powdered Sucanat (finely ground in coffee grinder)
2 tablespoons Agave Nectar

Crust Instructions:
1. Pulse walnuts and Brazil nuts in food processor until coarsely chopped.
2. Chop dates and add to food processor with coconut butter.
3. Process until well blended.
4. Press into two 4-inch tart shells. Crust should be ¼-inch thick all around.

Filling Instructions:
1. Process cashews, young coconut flesh, and coconut water in food processor until well blended.
2. Add lemon juice, agave, coconut butter, scraped insides from vanilla bean, and one banana.
3. Continue to process until light, fluffy, and very well processed.
4. Transfer to bowl and add second banana, sliced. Stir to combine.
5. Refrigerate for 30 minutes.
6. Remove from refrigerator, spoon into crusts, and sprinkle with leftover crust mixture and dried coconut.
7. Top with melted raw chocolate.

Raw Chocolate Instructions:
1. Melt cacao butter and coconut oil in dehydrator or over hot water.
2. In food processor, combine melted cacao butter, coconut oil, and vanilla extract.
3. Remove ½ of the mixture and set aside.
4. Add ½ cacao powder and combine.
5. Add Sucanat and combine.
6. Add remaining coconut butter mixture and combine.
7. Add remaining cacao powder; mix well. Chocolate should be quite liquid at this point. It will harden as it cools.

Pecan Pie

Chocolate and pecans make a great flavor combination. The pecan filling, combined with the whole pecans and maple syrup, give this pie a wonderful depth.

Serves 6–8

Crust:
2 cups Almonds, finely ground
¼ cup Cacao Powder
¼ cup Coconut Butter

2 cups halved Pecans, soaked until soft
½ cup Agave Nectar
$^1/_3$ cup Coconut Butter, softened

Topping:
½ cup Maple Syrup
¼ cup Coconut Butter, softened
1 cup Pecans

Crust Instructions:
1. Combine finely ground almonds with cacao powder and coconut butter.
2. Press into two 4-inch or one 8-inch tart pan with removable bottom.

Filling Instructions:
1. Combine soaked pecans, agave, and coconut butter in food processor.
2. Blend until smooth. You will need to scrape down the sides of the bowl.

Topping Instructions:
1. Whisk together maple syrup and coconut butter.

Assembly:
1. Fill tart crust with filling.
2. Top with pecans.
3. Pour topping mixture over pecans.
4. Refrigerate to set.

Apple Pie

Reminiscent of Grandma's Apple Pie, this recipe will become a staple in your raw food dessert collection. Loved by everyone, whether they eat raw or not!

Serves 4–6

Crust Ingredients:
2 cups Walnuts, soaked until soft
2 tablespoons Coconut Butter
1 tablespoon Agave Nectar

Maple Cinnamon Glaze:
1 tablespoon Coconut Butter, softened
3 tablespoons Maple Syrup
½ teaspoon Cinnamon

Filling:
4 Apples, peeled, cored, and thinly sliced
½ Lemon, juice from
¼ cup Maple Syrup
¼ cup Agave Nectar
1 teaspoon Cinnamon
⅓ cup Raw Oat Flour

Crust Instructions:
1. Drain walnuts. Place in food processor and process until a coarse meal is achieved.
2. Add coconut butter and agave. Process until well mixed.
3. Press ¼-inch thick into tart shells or 9-inch pie plate.
4. Dehydrate for 3 hours at 115°F. You can start at 140°F for 45 minutes and then lower the temp.

Filling Instructions:
1. Place apple slices in bowl.
2. Sprinkle with lemon juice and toss.
3. Mix together maple syrup, agave, and cinnamon.
4. Stir into apple mixture.
5. Add oat flour and toss to coat.
6. Place filling into two separate glass pie plates.
7. Place in dehydrator and dehydrate for 6 hours at 115°F, stirring occasionally. Add water if mixture starts to dry out.

Maple Cinnamon Glaze Instructions:
1. Whisk all ingredients together to combine.

Assembly:
1. Place filling in four 4-inch tart shells or one 9-inch pie plate that you have already prepared with the crust.
2. Remove from tart pan and top with Maple Cinnamon Glaze.

Strawberry Coconut Cream Pie

A beautiful, light-as-a-cloud strawberry pie with a surprise chocolate layer.
Perfect for your spring and summer table.

Serves 6–8

Crust Ingredients:
½ cup Macadamia Nuts
1 cup Almonds
2 tablespoons Coconut Oil, softened
½ cup Dried Coconut, finely shredded
2 tablespoons Agave Nectar

Filling:
1 Young Thai Coconut, flesh and ¼ cup liquid
2 cups Cashews, soaked for 3 hours
1 Vanilla Bean
¼ cup Coconut Oil
2 cups sliced, Strawberries
Large Flaked Dried Coconut

Chocolate Sauce:
1 Vanilla Bean
½ cup Cacao Powder
½ cup Agave Nectar
¼ cup Coconut Oil (melted over warm water)

Crust Instructions:
1. Place macadamia nuts and almonds in food processor. Process until a coarse meal is achieved.
2. Add coconut oil, shredded coconut, and agave. Pulse until blended.
3. Spread into an 8-inch pie plate. The crust will be sticky, so it helps to do this with wet hands.
4. Spread layer of chocolate filling.

Chocolate Sauce:
1. Split vanilla bean in half and scrape all the seeds out of the inside of the bean.
2. Place the vanilla bean seeds and the rest of the ingredients into the a high-speed blender.
3. Blend for 2 minutes.
4. Place in refrigerator to set.

Filling Instructions:
1. Split open the young coconut and reserve ¼ cup liquid. Scrape out the filling.
2. Place all ingredients except strawberries in a high-speed blender Process until smooth.
3. Place filling in bowl and stir in sliced strawberries.
4. Spoon filling into chocolate-lined crust, top with flaked coconut, and refrigerate until set.

Chocolate Raspberry Ganache Tart

This is a rich, decadent, and very easy to make dessert that will satisfy any chocolate (and raspberry) craving!

Serves 8–10

Crust Ingredients:
½ cup Macadamia Nuts
1 cup Almonds, soaked at least 6 hours
2 tablespoons Coconut Oil, softened
½ cup Dried Coconut, finely shredded
2 tablespoons Agave Nectar

Ganache Ingredients:
1 cup Cacao Powder
1 cup Agave Nectar
½ cup Coconut Butter, softened

Assembly:
1 pint Fresh Raspberries
Crust
Ganache

Instructions:
1. Combine all crust ingredients. Set aside.
2. Combine all ganache ingredients, whisk until smooth.
3. Pat crust into 9-inch tart pan with removable bottom.
4. Place a thick layer of raspberries on top of crust.
5. Spoon ganache over berries.
6. Refrigerate.

ICE CREAM, SORBET & FROZEN TREATS

Raspberry Sorbet

Lemon Ginger Sorbet

Cinnamon Plum Sorbet

Coffee Hazelnut Ice Cream with
Chocolate Ganache

Chocolate Cherry Ice Cream

Tropical Ice Cream

Making Ice Creams and Sorbets

Always chill your mixture before you make your ice creams and sorbets. It will make the freezing time shorter and also help your ice cream maker run more efficiently. Electric ice cream makers will only freeze your ice cream to "soft-serve" state. Transfer the ice cream into a container and make sure you give it a few stirs while it continues to freeze in the freezer.

Raspberry Sorbet

A simple, refreshing sorbet, bursting with the flavor of fresh raspberries.

Makes 2 cups

Ingredients:
2 pints Fresh Raspberries
½ cup Agave Nectar
1 teaspoon Fresh Lemon Juice

Instructions:
1. Puree raspberries in food processor and strain out seeds.
2. Stir agave into raspberry puree.
3. Freeze in ice cream maker, following manufacturer's instructions.
4. You can also freeze this in the freezer, occasionally scraping and stirring the mixture as it freezes.

Lemon Ginger Sorbet

Lemon, ginger, and mint combine for a crisp and oh-so-cooling summertime treat.

Makes 2 cups

Ingredients:
3 Lemons, juice and zest from
2 cups Water
2 tablespoons Ginger, grated
2 tablespoons Fresh Mint Leaves, minced
½ cup Agave Nectar

Crust Instructions:
1. Zest and juice lemons.
2. Combine lemon juice, lemon zest, water, grated ginger, minced mint, and agave.
3. Leave in refrigerator overnight to meld flavors.
4. Strain.
5. Freeze in ice cream maker, following manufacturer's instructions.
6. You can also freeze this in the freezer, occasionally scraping and stirring the mixture as it freezes.

Cinnamon Plum Sorbet

I love using plums right off the tree for this one. The addition of cinnamon fills out this tasty sorbet.

Makes 2 cups

Sorbet Ingredients:
Note: Make sure to only use the inside of the plums, as the skin is quite tart.
2 cups Plum Puree (the insides)
½ cup Agave Nectar
1 cup Almond Milk
½ teaspoon Cinnamon
Pinch of Salt

Almond Milk Ingredients:
1 cup Almonds, soaked at least 6 hours, drained
4 cups Water, filtered
2 Pitted Dates
1 Vanilla Bean, (the scraped insides)

Almond Milk Instructions:
1. In a high-speed blender combine almonds, filtered water, dates, and vanilla bean.
2. Process for 2 minutes. Strain through nut milk bag or several layers of cheesecloth.
3. (OPTIONAL) You can save the remaining pulp, dehydrate it, and use it as flour for other recipes.

Sorbet Instructions:
1. Make almond milk.
2. Place all ingredients in blender and blend until smooth.
3. Freeze in ice cream maker, following manufacturer's instructions. You can also freeze this in the freezer, scraping occasionally and stirring as it freezes.

Coffee Hazelnut Ice Cream with Chocolate Ganache

Though coffee is not raw, it is only a small part of this delicious confection—drizzle with chocolate ganache (page 115) for a quick trip to Heaven!

Makes 2 cups

Ingredients:
1 cup Hazelnuts
2 cups Coffee
½ cup Agave Nectar
½ cup Cashews, soaked until soft

Instructions:
1. Process hazelnuts and coffee together in high-speed blender until smooth.
2. Strain through nut milk bag or layers of cheesecloth.
3. Blend coffee-hazelnut milk, agave, and cashews in high-speed blender until smooth.
4. Freeze in ice cream maker according to manufacturer's directions. You can also freeze this in the freezer, scraping occasionally and stirring as it freezes.

Chocolate Cherry Ice Cream

I love the combination of chocolate and cherries. This refreshing ice cream is rich yet fresh. Use fresh cherries, when they're in season, for a wonderful treat.

Makes 3 cups

Ingredients:
½ cup Cashew Cream (see page 117)
2 cups Almond Milk (see page 83)
½ cup Cacao Powder
½ cup Agave Nectar
1 cup Cherries, pitted and sliced into quarters

Instructions:
1. Place all ingredients except cherries in high-speed blender. Blend well.
2. Freeze in ice cream maker according to manufacturer's directions. You can also freeze this in the freezer, scraping occasionally and stirring as it freezes.
3. Stir in cherries when ice cream is frozen but still soft.

Tropical Ice Cream

One of my favorite summer ice creams combines the flavors of the tropics. I am sure you will love this as much as I do!

Makes 4 cups

Ingredients:
2 cups Almond Milk (see recipe on page 83)
½ cup Cashew Cream (see page 117)
1 Young Thai Coconut, flesh from
1 cup Coconut Water, from a young coconut
¾ cup Agave Nectar
½ cup Pineapple, diced
½ cup Banana, sliced
½ cup Pecans, chopped

Instructions:
1. Place almond milk, cashew cream, coconut pulp, coconut water, and agave in high-speed blender. Blend until smooth.
2. Freeze in ice cream maker according to manufacturer's directions. You can also freeze this in the freezer, scraping occasionally and stirring as it freezes.
3. Stir in pineapple, banana, and pecans when ice cream is frozen but still soft.
4. Place in freezer to finish freezing.

Storage and Storage Containers

I am often asked: How long does this recipe keep? Can it be frozen? How should I store it? Here are a few common-sense rules you can follow:

1. If you would refrigerate the ingredients in the recipe, refrigerate the finished product. Biscotti, cookies, and other "dry" desserts freeze well. They will lose flavor and nutrients as time passes, but you can certainly extend their lives a bit by freezing.

2. I store my desserts and ingredients in glass containers with plastic snap-on lids. As more and more information comes out about plastics leeching chemicals into foods, I want to be safe, not sorry. For this reason, I don't let the food touch the plastic tops.

CONFECTIONS

Chocolates
Cacao Walnut Fudge
Hazelnut and Mint Truffles
Chocolate Covered Strawberries
Cinnamon Ginger Truffles
Doughnut Holes

Online Shopping

Items like cacao powder, raw cacao butter, coconut oil, and coconut butter can be found at great prices online. If you do your research, you can find great deals. Don't let the shipping charges stop you. Think about what your time, wear and tear on your car, etc. is worth and those shipping charges won't be an issue. You can find all of these ingredients in the "Store" at Rawmazing.com.

Chocolates

This versatile, basic recipe yields a hard, raw chocolate that's just sweet enough. Pure chocolate rapture.

Makes 2 cups

Ingredients:

7 ounces Raw Cacao Butter

$^1/_3$ cup Sucanat, ground fine in coffee grinder (make sure you grind the Sucanat fine or it will make the chocolate gritty)

2 cups Cacao Powder

3 tablespoons Agave Nectar

Instructions:

1. Melt cacao butter in dehydrator.

2. Place in food processor.

3. Add Sucanat, half of the cacao powder, and agave. Process until smooth.

4. Add the rest of the cacao powder and process until smooth.

5. Pour into molds or store for future use.

Cacao Walnut Fudge

A quick little bite to satisfy those chocolate cravings.

Makes 64 1-inch pieces

Fudge Ingredients:
1 cup Almond Butter
½ cup Cacao Powder
¼ cup Agave Nectar
½ cup Walnuts, chopped

Almond Butter Ingredients:*
2 cups Almonds (if making your own), or 1 cup Almond Butter

Fudge Instructions:
1. Make almond butter.
2. Mix together almond butter, cacao powder, and agave. It is easiest to do this with your hand.
3. Mix in the walnuts.
4. Press into an 8 x 8 square pan or use a mold. I used a little heart-shaped silicone mold.
5. Refrigerate for at least 2 hours.

Almond Butter Instructions:
1. Place almonds in food processor. Process, scraping down the sides of the bowl as needed.
2. The almond butter will take 6–12 minutes to form, passing through several stages: beginning as a coarse meal, then forming a ball, then spreading out and becoming smooth. Finally, as the oils are released, the almond butter will become shiny.
3. Be patient. The butter heats up but never gets over 100°F. Makes 1 cup of almond butter.

* You can find detailed almond butter instructions at www.rawmazing.com.

Hazelnut and Mint Truffles

These are more labor intensive than some of the other recipes but well worth the effort. Amazing in their taste and texture, they make great gifts!

Makes 2 dozen

Filling:
1 cup Cashews, soaked at least 3 hours
¹/₃ cup Agave Nectar
1 cup Dried Coconut, unsweetened

Mint Filling:
½ teaspoon Peppermint Extract

Filling Instructions:
1. Place drained cashews and agave in food processor. Process until smooth.
2. Add dried coconut and mix until well combined. A ball should form.
3. Remove ½ the filling mixture and set aside. You will be making two different fillings.

Hazelnut Filling:
1. Add hazelnuts to ½ of your filling mixture and process until nuts are chopped fine and mixture is well combined. Refrigerate for ½ hour.

Mint Filling:
1. Add peppermint extract to the second ½ of your filling mixture and mix well. Refrigerate for ½ hour.

Hazelnut Filling:
½ cup Hazelnuts, soaked for at least 3 hours and drained

Chocolate:
See page 97

Assemble the Truffles:
1. Roll both flavors of filling into 1-inch balls and place in freezer for 1 hour.
2. While filling is setting up, make the raw chocolate coating.

Final Assembly:
1. Take a filling ball and place a toothpick in it.
2. Dip ball in melted raw chocolate coating.
3. Holding the chocolate-dipped ball over the chocolate, let the extra chocolate run off. This may take some patience as you slowly turn the ball to get better coverage.
4. Holding the chocolate-covered ball upright, slide just the tip of a fork under the ball, and very carefully slide the ball onto a nonstick sheet. Repeat until all filling balls are covered. Return to refrigerator to set chocolate.

Chocolate Covered Strawberries

What a tasty way to enjoy chocolate and strawberries! Be sure to pick good, ripe strawberries.

Makes 2 dozen

Ingredients:
1 Recipe for Chocolate (see page 97)
2 pints Fresh Strawberries

Instructions:
1. Wash and dry strawberries and set aside.
2. Gently melt raw chocolate in dehydrator or over hot water.
3. Dip each strawberry in melted raw chocolate and set on serving plate.
4. Let cool.

Cinnamon Ginger Truffles

Originally made to take on a trip, these flavorful little bites travel well and delight even non-raw eaters!

Makes 2 dozen

Ingredients:
2 cups Almonds
1 tablespoon Cinnamon
1 teaspoon Ginger
½ teaspoon Nutmeg
¼ teaspoon Cloves
½ cup Dried Cranberries
½ cup Golden Raisins
½ cup Agave Nectar

Optional Ingredients:
Dried Coconut
Cacao Powder

Instructions:
1. Place almonds in food processor and process until finely ground.
2. Add spices and combine.
3. Add cranberries and raisins. Process for 5 seconds.
4. Add agave and process until well blended.
5. Roll into balls. This is sticky, so wetting your hands will help. They will set up when chilled.
6. Roll in dried coconut or cacao powder for more variations.
7. Refrigerate.

Doughnut Holes

Originally made to satisfy a doughnut craving, these flavorful little bites travel well and are a great sweet, healthy snack when the mood strikes!

Makes 2 dozen

Doughnut Ingredients:
2 cups Brazil Nuts
½ cup Oat Flour (made from raw oats)
1 cup Raw Flaked Oats
$^1/_3$ cup Coconut Oil, softened
$^1/_3$ cup Maple Syrup

Topping:
$^1/_3$ cup Sucanat
1 ½ teaspoons Cinnamon

Doughnut Instructions:
1. Prepare topping.
2. Process Brazil nuts in food processor until finely chopped.
3. In large mixing bowl, combine dry ingredients.
4. In separate bowl, combine wet ingredients.
5. Add dry mixture to wet and stir.
6. Form into 1-inch balls, rolling in topping to coat.
7. Set on serving platter.

Topping Instructions:
1. Combine Sucanat and cinnamon and put through blender.
   I use a coffee grinder to break up the grainy Sucanat.
2. (OPTIONAL) You can skip step 1 and just combine the ingredients.

Step 5

Step 6

Enjoy

BASICS

Why Young Coconuts?

In raw food recipes, the young coconut is a healthy substitution for many of the dairy products that we have eliminated. Recent research has found that the saturated fat contained in coconut actually protects against heart disease, stroke, and hardening of the arteries. Coconut oil contains large amounts of lauric acid, which is the main fatty acid found in breast milk. Lauric acid strengthens the immune system and protects against viral, bacterial, and fungal infections. Coconut flesh, coconut oil, and coconut butter are healthy substitutions.

Vanilla Custard

A versatile vanilla custard.

Makes 2 cups

Ingredients:
2 cups Cashews, soaked until soft
1 Young Coconut, flesh and ¼ cup liquid
¾ cup Coconut Butter, softened
½ cup Agave Nectar
1 Vanilla Bean

Instructions:
1. Split vanilla bean and scrape out insides.
2. Add to all other ingredients and process in a high-speed blender and process until smooth. You will have to be patient and use the plunger to get a really smooth consistency.
3. Refrigerate.

Chocolate Ganache

A rich chocolate ganache that will work many ways: as a frosting, a chocolate sauce, a fruit dip, and much more!

Makes 2 cups

Ingredients:
½ cup Agave Nectar
½ cup Cacao Powder
¼ cup Coconut Butter, softened

Instructions:
1. Whisk all ingredients together. It thickens more as it cools.

Cashew Cream

This cashew "cream" is amazingly versatile. Used as a base for our whipped cream, ice creams, and fillings, it stands in anywhere you would traditionally use cream.

Makes 3 cups

Ingredients:
2 cups Cashews, soaked overnight and drained
2 cups Water

Instructions:
1. Place cashews and water in high-speed blender and blend until smooth.
2. Refrigerate.

Cashew Whipped Cream

A denser whipping "cream" with great flavor.

Makes 1½ cups

Ingredients:
1 cup Cashew Cream (recipe on page 117)
½ cup Coconut Oil
¼ cup Agave Nectar

Instructions:
1. Blend all ingredients together.
2. Chill.

Caramel Sauce

A delightful caramel-like sauce that can be used to top many of the recipes! Try it on ice cream!

Makes 1½ cups

Ingredients:
½ cup Agave Nectar
½ cup Maple Syrup
¼ cup Coconut Butter, softened

Instructions:
1. Whisk all ingredients together.
2. Store in refrigerator.

STOCKING UP

There are a few things that I make sure I always have in my dessert pantry. If you open up my cupboard doors you will find the following:

Nuts

Almonds

Macadamia

Cashews

Flax Seeds

Brazil Nuts

Walnuts

Grains

Raw Oat Flour

Raw Oat Flakes

Other

Cacao Powder

Cacao Butter

Coconut Butter

Coconut Oil

Agave Nectar

Maple Syrup

Vanilla Beans

Vanilla Extract

Spices

Cinnamon

Ginger

INGREDIENTS

Agave One of my favorite sweeteners, agave is made from the sap of a cactus. It is low-glycemic with virtually no aftertaste, requiring only a small amount to do the job. Agave is available in various forms. I recommend the Xagave brand (see resources). If you don't want to use agave, choose a liquid sweetener of choice. Keep in mind that you want the same consistency.

Almonds A basic ingredient for raw desserts, almonds need to be soaked to release enzyme inhibitors.

Almond Flour There are two ways that you can make almond flour. You can place the almonds in the food processor and grind until fine, or you can dehydrate the leftover pulp from your almond milk and process the dried clumps until fine.

Avocados Containing almost twenty essential nutrients, including fiber, Vitamin E, B vitamins, and folic acid, avocados also help you absorb alpha- and beta-carotene and lutein.

Brazil Nuts With a mild flavor and creamy consistency, Brazil nuts make a beautiful nut milk. They can be substituted for almonds in many recipes—and are often less expensive. They have a high selenium content, and like other nuts, the fat is monounsaturated—the "good" fat—that's heart healthy. Brazil nuts contain copper, niacin, magnesium, fiber, and Vitamin E.

Cacao Nibs Partially ground cacao beans.

Cacao Powder With a high level of antioxidants, cacao powder is an excellent source of dietary fiber and is known to be one of the richest sources of magnesium. It contains an impressively high iron content and many other essential minerals in significant quantities, as well as B vitamins, which are essential for brain health. Cacao is also a source of serotonin, dopamine, and phenylethylamine, which are said to help alleviate depression and increase feelings of well-being. Cacao also contains anandamide, which delivers feelings of bliss. No wonder we love chocolate!

Cashews Like the other nuts, cashews are a good source of protein and fiber. They are also a good source of potassium, B vitamin, foliate, magnesium, phosphorous, selenium, and copper. It is extremely versatile in raw food recipes: spreads, "cheeses," cheesecakes, ice creams, dips, etc.

Cinnamon Coming from the brown bark of the cinnamon tree, cinnamon is antimicrobial, anti-inflammatory, and can help control blood sugar. Inhaling the scent is said to even increase brain function!

Young Coconuts Coconut flesh, coconut oil, and coconut butter are healthy substitutions. Recent research has found that the saturated fat contained in coconut actually protects against heart disease, stroke, and hardening of the arteries. Coconut oil contains large amounts of lauric acid, which is the main fatty acid found in breast milk. Lauric acid, strengthens the immune system and protects against viral, bacterial, and fungal infections.

Coconut Butter Made from coconut oil and coconut solids, coconut butter is not the same as coconut oil. It is richer in flavor and adds more depth of flavor.

Coconut Oil An edible oil coming from the coconut, coconut oil is not the same as coconut butter.

Dates Dates are the fruit of the date palm and are used for sweetening in some raw food recipes.

Dried Fruit You can dry your own fruit in the dehydrator or purchase it at your co-op. If it is sweetened, make sure that juice, not sugar, was used.
  Dried Cherries
  Dried Coconut
  Dried Apricots
  Dried Pineaple
  Dried Raisins
  Currants

Extracts Almond, vanilla, and peppermint extracts: Most extracts are alcohol based and not raw. I use them sparingly. You can find natural extracts on the web.

Flax A great source of Omega 3s and fiber, flax seed has many health benefits. There are two kinds of flax seed on the market: yellow and brown. In my recipes, I usually use yellow flax seed.

Fruit In fruit recipes, always choose fresh, ripe, unbruised fruit for the best possible outcome.

Ginger From the root of a flowering plant, ginger comes in powdered or whole form. It is used both ways in this cookbook.

Maple Syrup Not raw, but used frequently in raw food recipes, maple syrup has some health benefits and is far superior to sugar. It is used for flavor and texture.

Mint Fresh mint leaves can be found in the produce department in your grocery store.

Nutritional Yeast Though not raw, nutritional yeast is often found in raw food recipes. With a cheesy, nutty flavor it's a complete protein and is full of beneficial B vitamins. You can find it at your food co-op.

Nuts A key ingredient in raw food desserts, nuts are healthy and contain many nutrients for good health. Nuts are used for flour, in cream sauces, and more.

Raw Oat Flakes Super healthy, raw oat flakes are made simply by pressing the oat groat through a flicker. No heat or steam is used. The best ones come from Sunrise

Flour Mill.

Raw Oat Flour Made directly from organic oat groats, ground without heat processing, raw oat flour is one of my favorite ingredients for raw desserts. I get mine from Sunrise Flour Mills, where I know they source the best groats.

Salt Celtic sea salt or Himalayan sea salt are the best choices.

Spices Though most spices are not raw, they add flavor without impacting the health benefits.

Sucanat Not raw, but Sucanat is used in raw food recipes for its depth of flavor and consistency. It is dried sugar cane juice.

Sweet Orange Essential Oil Essential oil gives a great concentrated orange flavoring. Make sure you have a food-grade oil.

Vanilla Beans A great way to add natural vanilla flavor to recipes is to use vanilla beans. You split the beans and remove the insides.

NOTES

Even though Rawmazing recipes are made to be easy, some of the equipment and techniques in this book may be new to you. Take a minute to go over this quick list and many of your questions will be answered in advance. Raw desserts are nutrient and calorie dense. A little goes a long way. Serving sizes are smaller than traditional desserts. You can review and purchase most of this equipment at Rawmazing.com.

TOOLS

Food Processor: For making desserts quickly, a food processor becomes very important. It is great for making crusts, sauces, and simply mixing ingredients.

High-Speed Blender: I use a high-speed blender instead of a food processor when I want to achieve a super smooth consistency. Important when making custards and creamy sauces—and processing whole fruits and vegetables for smoothies and slushies—they're worth the investment. There are several models on the market—my preferred models are available at Rawmazing.com.

Dehydrator: Choose a dehydrator with removable shelves (so you can fit pie crusts inside) and temperature control. For instructions on dehydrating, see below.

Knives: Make sure you are always using sharp knives. It is well worth the investment.

Cutting Board: Bamboo cutting boards are my favorite these days. They are sustainable and don't dull your knives.

Microplane or Kitchen Rasp: Perfect for grating and zesting fruit peels. Available in several sizes.

Springform Pans: Made so you can release the sides, thus leaving the dessert free and clear when unmolding, springform pans are very important to have when making cheesecakes.

Tart Pans: Choose tart pans with removable bottoms to make it easier to get your beautiful desserts out of the pan and onto the plate.

Nut Milk Bag: Use a fine mesh bag to make nut milks. You can also use layers of cheesecloth.

TECHNIQUES:

Soaking Nuts: Certain nuts have enzyme inhibitors and require soaking to deactivate the enzymes and make the nuts more digestible. Some nuts are soaked to change their consistency for the recipes. I normally soak (in the refrigerator) and then dehydrate my nuts until dry as soon as I get them. If you need to soak just for consistency, plan on about 3 hours.

Dehydration: You may notice that some of the recipes start at a higher dehydration temperature. This can be confusing. We want to make sure that the food temperature stays below 116°F to ensure that raw enzymes stay intact.

But food temperature and air temperature are two separate things. We start at a higher temperature to speed up drying time and to prevent foods from fermenting. If you make sure to reduce the temperature in time, the food itself never gets above 116°F.

ABOUT THE AUTHOR
SUSAN POWERS

Susan Powers has always had a passion for the culinary arts. A trained sommelier, teacher, and accomplished cook with an eye for beautiful styling and articulated spice, she's studied and worked with many top chefs.

Learning classical French cooking along with the cuisines of many cultures inspired her love for rich, delicious foods. It also led her down the path to excess weight, general fatigue, and other physical symptoms including chest pain, joint pain, chronic heartburn, and constant fatigue. Sensing that her symptoms were associated with her diet, Susan began looking for a solution through food.

That's when Susan found raw. It was exciting to find a whole new way to prepare and eat food. The world of raw food was intriguing and creative, with new things to learn at every turn. She tried inventing recipes but was disappointed with the results. Once again she threw herself into the study of new techniques, using every raw foods cookbook she could find. As she learned to prepare the new dishes, she was reading about the health benefits of eating raw.

Her symptoms dissolved in a matter of days, and the weight melted off, but the benefits were far greater than that. She was experiencing a kind of mental clarity she'd never known. Life energy virtually pulsed through her body and her skin began to glow. Delighted and excited, Susan became 100% raw.

But all journeys have their bumps in the road. Minnesota winters are cold and long. Stress from other sources was building in Susan's life and she defaulted back to her "comfort food": rich, creamy desserts and buttery sauces, cooked potatoes and pastas.

This time, the difference in how she felt was unmistakable. Susan's own body had become the proving ground. As she gained back the weight she'd lost, grew fatigued, and lost focus, she knew she was at a moment of truth. When spring returned, Susan dedicated herself to raw again.

But this time, she did it differently. Now Susan focused on creating a raw foods repertoire that not only tasted wonderful and was beautiful to look at but also offered the "comfort" factor. Falling off the wagon had given her insight and a new question: Could a person achieve the same health results by eating 80–90% raw? She experimented with ways people might incorporate raw into their lives without becoming obsessed perfectionists.

Using her culinary training and natural creativity, Susan created a whole new raw: easy, beautiful food that tasted great and reminded her—and everyone she served it to—of the food they were accustomed to eating. Only this food tasted better!

As her confidence and expertise grew, Susan knew she'd discovered a cuisine and a lifestyle that could help the countless women and men who loved great food but struggled with health and weight issues.

In 2009, Susan launched Rawmazing.com, blogging about her experiments and posting her recipes.

Bringing traditional food preparation methods into the raw world, and balancing flavor, color, texture, and mouth feel, Susan introduced us to a whole new raw. Immediately her blog began to attract a loyal and vocal following.

Driven by their interest and her own high standards, intense creativity, and the most basic drive of all—a love of great food—Susan was able to translate family favorites into healthy, delicious—and remarkably easy-to-prepare—raw feasts.

Her own experience gives her a unique sensitivity to the journey from classical diet to raw, making her a sensitive, supportive teacher (cheerleader) to the tens of thousands of people who read her blog. I can't believe this is raw! her followers write. I fed this to my kids, to my husband—and they loved it!

This is Susan's unique gift to the raw food world. The ability to translate a formerly restrictive regimen, once the province of only the most extreme "foodies," to the American family table.

ONLINE RESOURCES

Raw Food Information and Recipes:
www.rawmazing.com

Our favorite raw oat and flour supplier:
www.sunriseflourmill.com

Xagave, our favorite, trusted agave nectar.
In my opinion, the best one out there:
www.xagave.com

The store at *Rawmazing*. You can find everything needed to
make these recipes here:
www.rawmazing.com